SERVICECRAFT

COUNTER SERVICE WORKBOOK

Nigel Hemmington
GLOSCAT

Series Editor: Roy Hayter, Hotel and Catering Training Board

M
MACMILLAN

First published 1988

Published by
MACMILLAN EDUCATION LTD
Houndmills, Basingstoke, Hampshire RG21 2XS
and London
Companies and representatives
throughout the world

Printed in Great Britain by
Scotprint Ltd, Musselburgh
British Library Cataloguing in Publication Data
Hemmington, Nigel
Servicecraft.
1. Hotel industries & catering industries.
Personnel. Training. Curriculum subjects:
Counter service of food & drinks — Manuals
I. Title
647'.95

ISBN 0–333–46337–4

CONTENTS

ACKNOWLEDGEMENTS

The publishers would like to express their sincere thanks to the following for their help with the photographs used in this book:

Barclays Bank plc (unit 5, photographer Keith Turnbull)
Catherine Blackie (picture research)
Cranks Wholefoods (unit 2, photographer Keith Turnbull)
Ford Motor Co. (unit 2)
Gardner Merchant Ltd (units 1 and 14)
Granada Motorway Services Ltd, Heston Services M4 (units 3, 8, 10, 11, 13, 14, 15, 16, 18 and 19, photographer Catherine Blackie)
Honeywell Bull Ltd, Hounslow (unit 4, photographer Keith Turnbull)
Instore Enterprises Ltd (unit 3)
London Tara Hotel (unit 7, photographer Catherine Blackie)
Lucas CAV, Acton, London W3 (units 9, 10, 11, 15, 16, 17 and 20, photographer Catherine Blackie)
Mecca Leisure Group plc (unit 8)
Sheraton Skyline, Hayes (units 9, 12 and 19, photographer Alexia Cross)
Sutcliffe Catering (South) Ltd (at Honeywell Bull and Lucas CAV)
Transmedia (cover photograph)
Travellers Fare Ltd (units 8 and 18)
Trusthouse Forte Welcome Break Service Areas (unit 6, photographer Elm Studios Ltd)

The publishers are grateful for the major contribution made by Jennifer Kimber (freelance writer), Mary James and Gill Verstage to the final text of this book.

ABOUT THIS BOOK

The aims of the book

This book is concerned with the basic procedures involved in the various forms of food service where customers help themselves, or are served from a counter, buffet table, carvery or vending machine, and take their food and drinks to a table or elsewhere.

Table service is dealt with in the companion title *Servicecraft: Table Service Workbook* and a third title, *Servicecraft: Food and Beverage Service*, deals comprehensively with the theory and takes many of the issues explored in this Workbook to greater depth.

As in all the Mastercraft books and their supporting videos, particularly *Servicecraft 2: Counter Service* and *Customercraft: Keeping the Customers Satisfied*, the emphasis is on meeting customers' needs.

How the book works

The material is organised in a series of self-contained units, each covering a double page opening or spread. The units can be read in any order—indeed the layout is designed to encourage the reader to 'dip into' the text at any point.

Each unit builds on core facts and know-how, showing the application of skills in the workplace and giving interesting and useful detail. The TO DO activity will help the reader draw together key information and apply it in a personal way.

The structure of the book

The different ways in which customers are informed of the choice of food and drink available, how they collect what they want and the equipment to eat it with are covered in the first units.

The methods by which food and drink are served, how they are protected from bacteria that might cause food poisoning and how they are paid for are other fundamental aspects of counter service. They are covered in unit 4. Units 5 and 6 explain how the design of self-service systems has been developed to reflect these issues. The automatic answer, vending machinery, is dealt with separately in unit 7.

The opportunities counter service provides for increasing food sales and the basic rules for displaying food attractively are covered in units 8 and 9. The final Insight unit, 10, looks at portioning.

The seven method spreads (units 11 to 17) follow the meal sequence: preparing for service, taking orders, serving food and beverages, clearing and taking payment. Customercraft is returned to in unit 18, covering personal hygiene, attitudes, behaviour and verbal skills, and dealing with complaints. Timing, working as a team, dealing with customers with special needs, and working safely and hygienically are the subjects of units 19 and 20.

1 THE CUSTOMER

Customers who can choose where to eat

Some customers eating a meal in a restaurant or cafeteria have been able to choose where they will go and what they will eat. As an example, take people who are out shopping. They want a meal because:

- They are hungry, but have more shopping to do and don't want to go home.
- They have the *money* to be able to afford to eat out.
- They have enough *time* available.
- Suitable eating places are *located* within easy reach and are *open*.

The decision of exactly where to go is likely to depend on:

- what *sort of food* they think they would like—a sandwich or a burger, a cold salad or a roast dinner
- how much *time* they feel they can spare
- what sort of *atmosphere* they are looking for—quiet and refined, bustling and jolly, trendy or old fashioned
- how much *money* they are willing to spend on the meal
- whether they *know and like* a particular restaurant, or have been recommended to try one
- how *far* they wish to walk or drive.

Customers who have no choice of where to eat

Some customers have no choice at all of where to eat. It may be because they are:

- working away from home and the meals have to be eaten in a dining room or canteen provided by their employer—for example, on an oil rig
- at a boarding school or residential college and all meals are paid for as part of the fees
- in hospital and confined to bed
- being taken care of in a home or institution and have no means of preparing their own food
- in prison.

Customers who have a limited choice of where to eat

There are probably more customers in this third group—people who do have some choice—for example:

- people working in an office or factory that has a staff restaurant, but where there is also a pub that serves food nearby
- train passengers who may use the buffet facilities at a station, or on the train, or may take their own food
- school pupils and college students who can make their own sandwiches for lunch, or go to the dining room or one of the inexpensive restaurants in the town
- car travellers who can choose somewhere to stop on their route, making a small detour if necessary (although on a motorway the most convenient option will be one of the motorway service areas).

What do food service customers expect?

When people are eating away from home, how satisfied they are with the food and service they receive depends on the following.

1. The quality of the food Wherever the customers are eating they will have certain expectations of the food they are ordering. These include:

- a certain quality of product
- well prepared food which looks and tastes good
- hot food served hot, cold food served cold.

2. Value for money Whether the establishment is a high class restaurant or a fish and chip shop, customers' satisfaction with what they receive will depend to some extent on the price they are charged. The value expected will vary from one customer to another, but generally all customers will want to feel they have had their money's worth.

3. Pleasant surroundings The physical environment of the restaurant, which is influenced by

- the decor, including the furniture, lighting, and music
- the cleanliness and standards of hygiene,

is only one factor in producing the expected environment for the customers, equally important is the quality of service.

4. The quality of service The level of service expected will depend partly on the price the customers are paying, on the standards they have experienced in other restaurants, and even on their mood. Generally if it is

- attentive and efficient
- friendly and welcoming, but not too familiar
- helpful, especially in advising on the selection of food and beverage

then their expectations will be met.

SERVICE TIPS

To provide good service you should:

- Smile and be friendly.
- When talking to each customer, give your undivided attention and establish eye contact.
- Show skill and efficiency when serving.
- Know the ingredients of the dishes, and how they are cooked.
- Make a good impression on the customers by presenting a clean and pleasant appearance.
- Show respect for your colleagues and help them to provide a good service.

How can customer expectations be met by the serving staff?

The members of serving staff are in effect selling the food, beverages and services of the establishment. They are involved in helping to create a pleasant and appropriate atmosphere, mainly by finding out what the customer needs and wants and then providing it.

The advantages of counter service for customers

- Speed—because the food and drink are usually prepared in advance, or may be prepared quickly, the customers can be served as soon as they have made a choice. In contrast to table service, there is no need for the serving staff to seat the customers, take the order and serve the meal.
- Display—food items may be displayed in an attractive manner which helps the customers in deciding which dishes to choose.
- Lower prices—it is possible to charge lower prices as fewer serving staff are required for counter service than for table service, and the cost savings may be passed on in lower meal prices.
- Choice—customers may make up their own meals from a choice of items, taking as much or as little as they want.
- Informality—the atmosphere is usually more informal, customers have the freedom to sit where they wish and to take as long as they like over the meal.

SERVICECRAFT

See *Servicecraft: Food and Beverage Service* and video 2: *Counter Service*

The disadvantages of counter service for customers

- Queues—large numbers of customers may require serving in busy periods, for example between 12 and 2 o'clock, resulting in long queues.
- Presentation—when customers are serving themselves from a counter, the appearance of the food will become less attractive during busy periods when the serving staff cannot check it frequently.
- Hygiene—some customers may touch food, for example bread rolls or fruit, that they do not personally require—such items are often wrapped or pre-plated to avoid this.
- Noisy or untidy dining areas—during busy periods this can be a difficult problem for serving staff to deal with, particularly if large parties of children or football fans are enjoying themselves!

TO DO

Where can shoppers have a meal or a snack in your local area? Make a list of the choices available and what you think would be the advantages and disadvantages for a mother who has her two young children with her.

Counter service is a style of food service where the food and drink is collected by the customer from some form of counter:

- A *display counter*, where plated and unplated food items and drinks are displayed, often behind transparent screens.
- A *service counter* in front of an illustrated menu, from which the customer makes a choice.
- A *buffet table*, or open counter on which food is displayéd and from which food is served.
- A *carving table* or counter where roast meats are carved and served.
- A *hotplate*, a heated surface holding food containers.
- A *vending machine* dispensing from a display of wrapped food, tinned or bottle drinks, or mixing hot and cold drinks selected from a list on the front.

Having chosen their meal from the counter, the customers then either take it to the dining area to be eaten or take it away to be consumed later. In some cases the customers may sit at the counter to eat the meal.

These forms of counter are all associated with particular styles of counter service. There are also some adaptations where the principle remains true: that customers come to the food.

> *** FOR INTEREST**
>
> In *table service* everything is brought to the customers at their table, either carried from the kitchen on the plate from which it will be eaten (that is, *plated*) or carried from the kitchen on a serving dish and transferred to the customers' plates in their view.

Self-service counters

On the counter, or counters, are displayed the different food and drink items. Hot dishes are kept in heated cabinets, cold foods such as salads and sweets are kept in chilled cabinets, while items which should be kept at room temperature, for example biscuits and bread rolls, are either placed on display shelves above the cabinets or put in their own display cabinet.

The customers collect a tray then move along the counter selecting the items to make up their meal. There may be one long counter with the selection in menu order but also arranged so that hot food will not get cold, or there may be a number of separate counters displaying particular ranges of food and drink so that customers need only go to the counters they are interested in.

In situations where the meal has to be paid for, the payment point is located at the end of the counter or on the way to the dining area. Cutlery, napkins and sauces are placed at a convenient point so that customers who return to collect items can do so without needing to pass by the payment point again, or join a queue.

Either some or all the meal items may be served from behind the counter by the serving staff (*partly* or *fully-assisted* service) or the customers may help themselves to everything (*un-assisted service*).

Usually, hot items, main courses and hot beverages are served by the serving staff. Beverages may also be dispensed from a vending machine.

Self-service counters are commonly used in restaurants at motorway service areas, airport terminals, department stores, offices and factories, schools, colleges and universities.

> *** FOR INTEREST**
>
> *Mobile catering services* range from small hand-pushed hot dog stands to fully equipped vehicles selling a range of cooked meals, including fish and chips, and burgers. The vehicles may be permanently sited, such as in road lay-bys, or may be on the move, stopping when requested by customers, such as ice-cream vans.
>
> *Drive in service* is popular in the USA. The customers drive up to a service point on the outside wall of the restaurant to collect the assembled meal, usually fast food items such as burgers. The order is taken through an intercom, further down the queue. Drive-in service can take another form, when the food is brought to the customers who remain in their cars.

Fast-food service

The customers order and collect their meals from one of a number of service points along the service counter. At each of the service points there is a cash till and a member of staff who takes the order, receives the payment, collects the meal items and assembles them on a tray to be eaten in the restaurant, or in a bag or container to be eaten away from the restaurant. This type of service is most suitable where there are a limited number of menu items and there is no need for the food to be displayed. The food is usually shown in photographs alongside the menu above the counter.

Many take-away restaurants, such as fish and chip shops and Chinese take-aways, use a similar method but only have one service point behind the counter.

Buffet service

Customers select meal items from an open counter or table on which the food is displayed. The attractive presentation of food is a major feature of buffets. Sometimes they are deliberately designed to tempt customers to order from the cold selection (perhaps because this will relieve the pressure on the kitchen staff). On other occasions they help sell the restaurant or hotel by showing off the talents of the kitchen staff. The organisers of functions also like them because an impressive display means they have chosen the venue well, a feeling of abundance is created, yet the costs may well be lower than a fully-served sit-down meal.

The customers either help themselves to everything, or the serving staff serve all (or some) of the items.

Buffet service is suitable for small and large functions (for example, business meetings and weddings) where a reasonably informal atmosphere is sought and fast service is required without the need for large numbers of serving staff.

Buffets are a popular means of speeding up the service of breakfast in hotels, at the same time providing a wider selection of cereals, fruit juices and hot dishes than is often practicable with full table service.

USEFUL TERMS

Fork buffet The food is of the sort (or cut into small pieces) that can be eaten with a fork only, the other hand then being free to hold the plate (there is usually limited seating).

Finger buffet The food is served in small pieces, suitable for eating without the need for cutlery.

Cover Another name for the place setting (cutlery, napkin, crockery, wine glasses). Can also refer to the number of customers served.

Accompaniments Items which are served with the main dish, for example, sauces, toast, lemon wedges.

Carvery service

The starter and sweet are served by the serving staff, and the customer collects the main course items from the carving table where the joints of meat are displayed, kept hot by special lamps mounted above, and hotplates below.

Often a chef is on duty from the kitchen to carve the joints to the customer's requirements, but sometimes a member of the serving staff does the carving and in some restaurants the customers can carve for themselves. Usually customers help themselves to vegetables, gravy, sauces and other accompaniments such as Yorkshire pudding. Carveries are popular in some busy restaurants and particularly for the service of Sunday lunch.

Seated counter service

The customers are seated at the counter, usually on stools, and are served by staff behind the counter. The place settings are laid up and cleared in front of the customers and meal items are served as the customers request them. Sometimes some of the food preparation is done in view of the customers, at the counter, or in the central island provided by U-shaped counter arrangements. Preparation staff may then also serve.

Seated counter service is often used in situations where customers are likely to be on their own, for example railway stations and airport terminals (this is especially true in the USA and Europe).

Vending service

This consists of a mechanical dispenser of products, such as confectionery, drinks, packaged snacks or even whole plated meals. The items can be obtained at any time of the day or night, and serving staff are only needed to replenish and clean the machines, not to serve.

Vending machines are found in underground and railway stations, airport terminals, hotels, pubs and other public places where they are coin-operated. They are also found in offices, factories and staff dining rooms where they are sometimes operated by a special disc or card issued to the staff, or simply at the press of a button (free vend).

TO DO

Make a list of at least five counter service style restaurants you know of. Note as many details as you can of:

- the way in which the food is displayed
- how the counters are arranged (it may help to draw a rough plan)
- the extent to which the staff are involved in the service of the food.

The way in which customers collect their food and drink, whether the choice they have needs to be explained with a menu, and how they collect the equipment necessary to eat the meal are fundamental aspects of all styles of food service.

Served or self-service

If the food is to be served by staff at the counter, then it is better for the staff to stand on the other side of the counter from the customers. In this way movement of both staff and customers can occur independently, without the one hindering the other. Staff can have easy access to the kitchen to replenish food supplies, and to storage areas.

When the food is served it may be completely protected from the customer by glass screens, with a shelf at the top for passing through the plated food. Food will be arranged so that it looks attractive from the customer side, but can be easily reached from the service side.

If the customers are going to help themselves to the food, then it is not unusual for the counter to be along one wall of the room, with no access from behind. The food is laid out so that it can all be easily reached by the customers, and dishes that are difficult to handle without the assistance of serving staff will tend to be avoided. When the buffet is for large numbers and dishes of food will have to be replaced during service, then it is better to have a gap between the back of the counter and the wall. Serving staff can them move empty dishes away and put down new dishes without inconveniencing the customers.

Customer movement at the counter

Where there is a very limited choice of food on the counter, then customers can go to just one point of the counter. For example, in a carvery where it is usual to offer a choice of three or four roast meats, these can all be set up on a small counter. The vegetables would usually be placed next to the meats or on another counter nearby, and the customer will have to move to that counter once the meats have been served.

The wider the choice of food and drinks the longer the counter surface required, and the greater the distance the customers will have to move through to see the selection and make their choice. The difficulty can then arise, particularly with large numbers of customers, that those who are looking at food and deciding what to have will hold up other customers behind them in the queue. The fact that some of these customers also may not require dishes at certain points in the display will not prevent them from having to move past them in the queue—unless the displays can somehow be broken into groups and customers be directed only to those they are interested in.

Fast food restaurants cope with busy periods by opening up sufficient service points along the counter, resulting in several short queues rather than one long one.

Buffet organisers' approach to the queuing problem is to set up a duplicate buffet arrangement, either on a separate table or occupying half of a very long table.

Food arrangement on the counter

The food items are usually arranged on the counter according to two criteria:

1. What temperature control is required. Most equipment for keeping food hot, chilled or frozen can only perform one of these functions, so hot food will be put together in one cabinet, cold items in another. However some equipment does have a suitable top surface for arrangements of items that can be kept at room temperature, and some counter units can keep cold food on the bottom shelf and hot food on the middle shelf.

2. What role the item is intended to play in the meal: simply a snack, a starter, the main course, a sweet, or a drink to accompany food. It is usual to try and arrange the food in the natural sequence of the meal, with the exception that hot items are placed towards the end of the selection so they do not get cold while other items are being chosen and served. There are sometimes other factors which influence where the food goes, for example high profit dishes may be placed early in the selection before customers have filled up their plates or chosen something else.

TO DO

Look at the way in which menus are used in two counter service restaurants of your choice. Consider their effectiveness as a customer.

- Are they located in a place where they can be easily read?
- Do they help customers to make their choice or is their role just to indicate the prices?
- What improvements would you suggest?

Menu

1. *Illustrated menu* A menu with pictures of the food items may be displayed behind the service counter. This is particularly useful where the customers cannot see the food items they are selecting, for example in fast food restaurants. The prices of the items are usually shown alongside the pictures.
2. *Wall board* A board giving descriptions of the items and their prices may be displayed at the start of the counter or behind it. Where there are different counters serving different food and drink items, a menu may be placed behind or above each counter, giving descriptions and prices for the items served at each.
3 *Table menu* Where the service is part-assisted or in buffet meals, menus may be placed on the tables at which the customers eat. The serving staff may take orders for part of the meal, for example, the main food item, and the customers serve themselves to salads and vegetables from a selection on a buffet table. The items may be priced separately or more usually there is a set price for the meal.
4. *No menu* In some situations, for example when a buffet is served at a function, there is no menu provided, the food items requiring no description. A price list will only be displayed if customers are not the guests of the organiser and are expected to pay.
5. *Individual item descriptions* Descriptions and prices may be placed on the counter alongside each of the different food items.

Eating equipment

In some counter service situations such as fast food restaurants, there is little or no cutlery provided. Straws, drink stirrers and napkins are placed on the service counter by the tills. In more formal restaurant situations and where part of the meal is served at the table by serving staff, the tables may be set with cutlery, side plates, glasses and napkins, before the customers enter the dining area.

Where customers are responsible for collecting their own cutlery and napkins, these are placed on another counter or table between the payment point and the dining area or sometimes in the dining area itself. Salt, pepper and sugar are sometimes the only things placed on the table in advance. Otherwise they are left with the cutlery, where sauces are also left (unless these are charged for by the sachet).

Methods of serving food

1. *Packet or box*—fast food and take-away restaurants pack the prepared food items in boxes or bags, the counter service staff produce the requested items ready packaged as the customer orders. The food items are precisely portioned to a standard size, for example a 100 g (4 oz) beef burger in a bread roll.
2. *Pre-plated*—portioned food items are placed on the plate in the kitchen, and then arranged on the counter to be selected by the customers. Pre-plated cold food items are often covered with a cellophane wrapper to protect the food and retain its freshness.
3. *Served by staff at the counter*—the food items are displayed on the counter in trays or containers, the counter service staff serve the items as the customer requests them. There is usually a standard portion size, for example one portion may consist of two scoops of mashed potato and two sausages.
4. *Self-served*—the customers help themselves to items from containers on the counter. Certain items may be priced individually, for example slices of pie, or per helping, for example salads. Customers can serve as much of any item as they wish, but pay for each slice of pie and each type of salad they choose.

Drinks service

In counter service situations, customers may serve their own hot and cold drinks or the drinks may be served by the counter service staff.

1. *Drink dispensers*

Automatic dispensers are used to dispense both hot and cold drinks. The machines may either be situated on the counter for the customers to serve themselves or behind the counter, the counter service staff serving the drinks to the customers' requirements. Hot drinks which may be served by this method include tea, coffee, and chocolate. Cold drinks include cola, orangeade and lemonade, orange squash and fruit juices.

2. *Bottles and cans*

Bottles and cans of cold drinks may be kept in the chilled cabinet on the counter. The customers select the item they want and place it on the tray with the rest of their meal. Cold drinks may also be served ready-poured in glasses (fresh fruit juice is often served by this method).

Alcoholic drinks, including beer and wine, may be served in bottles and cans. In some counter service restaurants wine may be served by the glass, already poured.

3. *Poured by serving staff*
Hot drinks may be made by the counter service staff and poured into cups as the customers request them. Tea and occasionally coffee may also be made in individual pots for the customers to serve themselves at the table.

4. *Served at the table*
Where the service is part-assisted, hot and cold drinks may be served to the customers at the table where they eat the food.

Hygiene

Hygiene is an extremely important consideration in any form of food service. In counter service, maintaining good standards of hygiene is especially important as customers may have to touch the food items to serve themselves, and are in close proximity to food which other people will be eating.

The different ways in which the food and drink is arranged and served at the counter call for different methods of protection:

- Pre-boxed—some counter service outlets serve the food in boxes and bags. The food items are placed in the containers in the kitchen. The counter service staff simply gather together the packaged items as the customers order them. The minimum number of people touch the food and hygiene is at a maximum.
- Protected by screens—many counters are protected by transparent 'sneeze screens'. These may be accessible from the customers' side of the counter, having flaps which the customers open when they require the item behind the screen. When the counter service staff serve the food to the customers, the screens provide a transparent wall to protect the food while still allowing customers to view the food items.
- Wrapped in cellophane—some food items may be wrapped in cellophane in the kitchen, for example sandwiches and portioned cakes. Plated meals, such as salads, may be given a cellophane covering to keep the items fresh and hygienic.
- No protection—in many counter service situations the food is displayed without protection, for example on buffet tables. It is then the duty of the serving staff to ensure that the customers do not need to touch the food more than necessary, by providing enough serving utensils and by presenting the food in a manner which allows the customers to pick up one portion without disturbing the next.

Handling money

In fast food outlets the counter service staff take the customer's orders, enter the items into the cash register, take the money and gather together the selection. The counter service staff may safely handle money as they never actually touch the food items.

Many counter service restaurants have a cashier who sits at a till beyond the food counters. Once the customers have chosen their meals they take the items to the till where the cashier totals the bill.

In some counter service establishments, for example fish and chip shops, the counter staff are involved in serving the food to the customers, taking the money and sometimes doing the cooking. Special care needs to be taken to wash hands thoroughly before food items are touched after money has been handled.

* FOR INTEREST

Cash registers

1. *Pre-programmed tills*—the tills are pre-programmed with the prices of individual items, the service staff enter the items required and the totalled bill is calculated by the machine.
2. *Cash registers*—the cashier is required to remember the prices of individual items or refer to a price list by the till. The prices of the food items are entered into the cash register and the totalled amount is calculated by the machine.
3. *Written bills*—the counter service staff are required to make up and total a written bill, entering the amount the customer has to pay into the cash register.

!! REMEMBER

Security

Security is important when handling cash, cheques, credit cards, or vouchers.

DO NOT:
- leave money lying around
- leave the till unattended
- leave the till drawer open
- carry large amounts of money around.

DO:
- check figures carefully
- hand over money as soon as possible.

TO DO

Write a brief report for your supervisor or tutor on how the food is priced in two establishments of your choice.
If possible include one where the customers help themselves from dishes or containers on the counter.

Include in your report details of what equipment, if any, is used for calculating the bill and taking payment. How did the cashiers know what prices to charge the customers?

5 INSIGHT

There are a number of ways in which counters may be arranged for efficient food service. The factors that need to be considered at the initial design stage for a purpose-built restaurant, or at the setting-up stage if it is a temporary arrangement for a function using buffet service include:

1. The style of counter service to be offered (see unit 2).
2. The number of customers expected and the pattern in which they are likely to arrive. At an office or factory canteen a known number of lunches may have to be served over a period of one or two hours, with no one person taking longer than 30 minutes for a meal, including queuing time at the counter. At a motorway service area the flow of customers may be more difficult to predict, on holiday routes the peak periods may be on Saturdays during the summer. On other routes changes in the weather may cause sudden peaks in traffic.
3. The staffing arrangements—how many staff will be available and what level of service the customers will expect. Of all forms of counter service, vending machines have the lowest staffing level and are therefore popular in locations and at times where the demand for food and drink is not sufficient to require special catering staff.
4. How much space is available, where it is in relation to delivery points, kitchens, storage areas, power and water supplies, and what other purposes, if any, the space has. If an existing area is to become the service area, then its shape will also have to be considered. Counter arrangements that are possible in spacious rooms are unlikely to suit long, narrow rooms.
5. What food and drinks will be offered and the choice that will be available. A limited selection of cold meats and salads or cocktail snacks will require less space than a full meal range, with a selection of hot and cold starters, main courses and sweets.

Counter arrangements

The main types of arrangement are:

- straight line counters, also known as single counters
- the variations on straight line counters:
  —double straight lines
  —straight line multiple access
  —multiple service points
  —open display
  —seated counter service
- multiple or staggered counters, also known as free flow or scramble systems
- carousel counters.

Straight line counters

This is the traditional counter arrangement used in cafeterias, but now a less popular choice than multiple counters (see unit 6). Tray rails run the length of the counter. The customers collect their trays at the start of the counter and move along the counter selecting food and drink items. These can be quickly placed on their trays, the tray rail taking the weight. Payment is taken at a till located at the far end of the counter.

Menu boards may either be placed at the start of the counter or located at each section. These boards will indicate the foods that are available and their prices.

This style of counter can serve between 4 and 8 customers per minute depending on the speed of the service staff, proficiency of the cashier, and the menu display, and the familiarity of the customers with the order of presentation of food and drink items.

Where the restaurant is serving complete meals it is important that there is some logical presentation of the items on the counter, so that customers can select a starter, main course, sweet and drink in the correct order.

USEFUL TERMS

Backfittings The hot-cupboards, shelves and other equipment behind the counter, from which staff collect food and drink items to replenish the counter or to serve directly to the customer.

Service area The area behind the counter where the staff work, including the backfittings and hatches/access to the kitchen.

Hot-cupboards Usually located below the counter, used for heating plates and for keeping reserve containers of food hot.

Bains-marie Used for keeping food hot. They usually form the top of hot-cupboards or the serving counter, and come with specially designed containers, made to fit into a water bath or hot air bath.

Hot lamps Special lights located above the counter that radiate heat down on to the food, helping to keep it hot.

Variations on straight line counters

Double straight lines This arrangement allows two queues of customers to be served at the same time. The counters may be arranged in various ways. Both may display the same types of meal item, or they may each display different types of foods, for example, one serving full meals and the other snacks.

There are three basic arrangements of double straight line counters:

1. One counter is divided into two, with both halves serving the same selection of items. Customers may start at either end and move towards the cash points located at the mid-point of the counter, or start at the mid-point and move towards either end.
2. Parallel counters, with the customer flow between the counters on either side.
3. Two counters run parallel to each other on either side of a central service area.

This method of counter arrangement is often used in very busy restaurants, serving a large number of customers at the same time, for example college canteens or airport restaurants.

Straight line, multiple access Straight line counters may be divided into sections serving different food and drink items, each with its own queue. Customers queue at the counter serving the items they require, then take their tray to one of the free-standing cash tills to pay, and eat their meal in a dining area beyond the counters. This type of counter arrangement has been largely replaced by staggered counters (see unit 6).

TO DO

Straight line counter arrangements are often used for meal service in schools. Discuss with your colleagues what the reasons for this might be and make your own list of the advantages and disadvantages.

Alternatively choose another situation where a straight line counter is used (for example, a local restaurant).

Other variations on straight line counters

Multiple service points The counter has a number of service points along its length, each manned by one or two members of the serving staff. The customers queue for service at any one of the service points, from where the orders are taken, the meal items assembled and payment received.

The kitchen area is behind the counter, the food preparation staff prepare and cook the food items and pass them through to the various dispensers and hot plates ready for service.

Open display This is usually a come-and-go-as-you-please arrangement. The food choice is explained on the menu handed to customers when they have sat down at their table. Alternatively the menu may be part of the table setting, or serving staff may explain the choice.

Open display can be used for the whole meal, or just to provide another choice for a particular course, when the other dishes are all brought to the table by the serving staff. An example of this limited use is at pizza restaurants where the first course can be chosen from a salad bar displayed near the front entrance (where it also helps to catch the eye of passers-by and stimulate the appetites of customers as they arrive). Another example is the carvery restaurant, where if customers choose a roast meat as the main course they get up from the table and choose their requirements at the carving table (see unit 2).

Where the full meal is available on an open display basis, hot foods will be served from hotplates or special warming dishes, and foods which need to be kept chilled are either kept on crushed ice or placed in special cabinets.

Seated counter service Where customers sit and eat their meals at the counter where they are served, the counter may be a single straight line, or it may be 'U' or even 'W' shaped, with a number of service bays around which customers sit. The serving staff take the customers' orders, pass them to the kitchen and collect the food from hatches behind the counter area.

Individual menus may be located on the counter or there may be a menu displayed behind the service area. Meals are usually plated and each bay is equipped with cutlery, crockery and condiments.

Seated counter service arrangements are popular in small bistros and snack bars, where the counter is in front of the food preparation area. The staff who prepare the food also serve it.

The islands in the centre of U and W-shaped counter arrangements are sometimes used to display some of the cold food items available, for example salads and sweets.

Multiple or staggered counters

These arrangements make use of a number of smaller counters offering different groups of meal items, for example separate counters for starters, salads, hot main courses, sweets and beverages. A menu board is located at each of the counters listing the food items on offer and the prices.

In the *free flow* or *scramble* system, as it is called, the customers can choose which counter or counters to go to, and collect the food they require quickly. At busy periods queues may still form at the most popular counter, or where the food is served (either by staff or self-served). However most customers find this a less frustrating experience than being held up in a queue by people in front of them making a selection they are not interested in. The flow of customers through the system will also get faster (as many as 15 per minute) in situations where the customers are familiar with the choices on offer and the service arrangements—as they would be in an office or works canteen.

There are three basic ways of arranging the counters.

Staggered
The counters are arranged at angles, usually facing towards the restaurant entrance so that customers have a good view as they walk in. This is also called an *echelon* or *saw-tooth* arrangement.

Hollow square
The counters are placed around the walls of a large service area, forming a square.

Shopping centre
Counters are placed more informally around the room, arranged as the counters are in many department stores.

In whatever counter arrangement is used, the customers proceed to the eating area via the payment point. The cutlery is also placed near the exit point, along with napkins, seasoning and sauces. The trays are placed near the entrance point and the counters have tray rails so that customers can rest the tray while they collect their food or drink.

Good signposting is important so that customers can quickly identify the counter holding the items they are interested in choosing.

Carousel counters

Carousel counters are circular and revolve slowly to display the items on offer. The counter is usually located so that one side is accessible to the kitchen or service staff, and the other side to the customers. As the carousel passes through the kitchen the food items are replenished. The customers stand by the counter on the dining side and select items as the carousel revolves slowly past them.

There may be three shelves on the carousel each displaying a different type of food:

- The lower shelf may be chilled and hold cold food items.
- The middle shelf may be heated (the heat rising away from the cold shelf).
- The top shelf is usually not temperature controlled and may hold items such as bread rolls and biscuits.

The food is usually plated and the choice may be fairly limited. It is then a suitable counter arrangement for achieving a high customer throughput (8 to 10 per minute) in limited space.

If a wider range of items needs to be offered, the carousel may be used for cold items and snacks only, while hot dishes are served from another, fixed counter. When a selection of salads is made available on a self-serve basis, these are not usually put in the carousel because some customers may have to stand by the counter for two or three revolutions to be able to get what they want.

TO DO

Visit a self-service restaurant near you which uses a free flow or scramble system. Study the arrangement of counters and then make a rough sketch indicating:

- the position of each counter
- what items are served at each counter
- where the trays are placed
- where the cutlery, napkins etc. are placed
- where the payment point is and how many cash tills are available.

Finally make an estimate of the number of customers that pass through in a minute—if possible during a busy time.

7 INSIGHT

Vending is the provision of food, drinks and other items in exchange for money or free of charge, from a machine that is operated by customers at the time they require the service:

1. Where payment is required the customer inserts the money, or in some situations a pre-programmed card is used.
2. The selection button for the required product is pressed.
3. The electronic controls of the machine release the product, which drops into a tray at the base of the machine. In some machines the customer opens a flap to obtain the product. In drinks machines a cup is released and the product is poured into the cup.

Advantages of vending operations

1. Convenience—food and drink can be provided 24 hours a day at the touch of a button. Customers who are working unsociable hours or those in a hurry can obtain what they want, when they want it and, perhaps when other food services are unavailable.
2. Predictability—the product is always produced to a standard quality and quantity.
3. Hygiene—from the moment the food or drink item is prepared and wrapped in protective packaging to the time the customer consumes it, it remains untouched by human hands.
4. Choice—a comprehensive vending operation will offer a range of food and drink items. Many machines have special features enabling customers to alter their choice to a specific requirement, for example drinks machines may allow extra milk or sugar to be added.

Location of vending operations Vending is an extremely versatile method of serving food and drink items, and can be used in many situations, from an air conditioned office to a street corner.

Examples of typical locations include:

- Offices, providing tea and coffee, snacks and sweets.
- Construction sites, where workers are in an isolated situation with no other service available. Hot and cold drinks, sandwiches and cigarettes, and full meals may be provided.
- Hotels: in bedrooms, where a 24 hour bar service is required, or in corridors where non-alcoholic drinks are provided.
- Airports, railway stations and bus stations, where passengers may have to wait for considerable periods and require catering services 24 hours a day.
- Hospitals, for customers waiting for appointments and visiting patients, and for the hospital staff who require refreshment while working long shifts.
- Motorway service stations, for travellers in a hurry who require an item at any time of the day or night.
- Pubs and clubs, for dispensing cigarettes and condoms.

Drinks vending

A drinks vending machine can cater for the needs of between 150 and 250 people a day, depending on the amount of use the customers make of it.

There are several ways that drinks are dispensed through a vending machine:

- *Premix*: the ingredients are combined in advance and kept in a liquid form ready for instant service. The method is only suitable for products with stable keeping qualities, for example fruit-flavoured soft drinks.
- *Post-mix*: the flavouring product is kept in concentrated liquid or powder form and then mixed at the point of service with hot water, iced still water or for fizzy drinks, iced carbonated water.

* FOR INTEREST

Main groups of items vended

Hot and cold drinks
Tea, coffee, chocolate, meat extract drinks, soup, still and fizzy drinks, milk, milkshakes.

Snacks and sweets
Crisps, nuts, biscuits, chocolate bars, sweets, fruit.

Hot and cold meals
Rolls, sandwiches, salads, pies, sausage rolls, hot plated meals, frozen or chilled meals.

Alcoholic beverages
Spirits, for example whisky, gin and brandy; canned or bottled beer and wine.

Other items
Newspapers and books, cigarettes, medical supplies.

* FOR INTEREST

Varieties of cups

Polystyrene
Retains the heat of the drink, does not burn the customer's hand.

Paper
Cardboard cups lined with plastic, cheap to produce, but difficult to hold.

Plastic
Similar to paper cups, may be used with a holder.

China cups
Not disposable, after use they are washed, dried and returned to the machine for reloading.

- *Fresh brew*: this method applies to tea and coffee, each individual cup being produced from tea leaves or from ground coffee at the time of sale. The machines are slower than other vending machines, but produce a superior product. A variation of this method uses tea or coffee bags and hot water.
- *In-cup*: pre-packaged in the cup in a concentrated powder form. Hot water has simply to be added to the cup at the point of sale.
- *Pre-packaged cartons, cans or bottles*: spirits, wines and beers, fresh fruit juices and milk are sold in this way. They are products which do not respond well to being reduced to a dehydrated or concentrated form.

Food vending

Machine vending snacks are found in a variety of locations, such as schools, offices and railway stations. They provide mostly 'brand name' items, which are sometimes specially packaged to fit the vending operation.

Some machines provide freshly produced snacks, such as sandwiches and rolls, either bought in from an outside caterer or made on the premises.

Full meal vending is only practical where a large number of customers are certain to use the machine. There are two main methods used:

- heated cabinets in which a pre-cooked and plated meal is held at a temperature of around 70°C (160°F) for a maximum of six hours
- refrigerated cabinets which hold pre-plated food at a low temperature:
  —around 4°C (40°F) for salads, cold meats etc.
  —just above freezing for foods produced in a cook–chill system for reheating when required (they are chilled to this temperature within a very short time of cooking and each stage of the operation is strictly supervised).

Reheating of food takes place in a microwave oven alongside the vending machine. Instructions on the packaged food will state how long it should spend in the oven. Some systems use a colour code system, for example a red dot would indicate that the red button on the oven timing control should be depressed. Even more sophisticated systems use tokens supplied with the meal. When inserted into the oven controls, the token automatically programs it.

Perishable foods cannot be left in vending cabinets for long periods, even if the cabinet is chilled. Chilled salads may lose their appearance after one day. Chilled meats, fish and egg dishes should never be kept longer than three days—and then only if there is no doubt about the machine's ability to maintain safe holding temperatures constantly.

* FOR INTEREST

Alcohol vending

A small number of vending machines are able to dispense alcoholic drinks, but their locations are restricted because of the licensing laws. These machines are often found in hotel rooms, for use by residents

- when the bar is closed,
- as an alternative to going to the hotel bar,
- instead of ordering from room service.

They normally dispense miniature spirit bottles or canned beer.

TO DO

Describe a vending machine that you have used. What food and drink items did it serve? Count the number of customers using the machine during a typically busy half-hour period.

8 INSIGHT

Promotion at the counter is concerned with influencing the decisions that customers make within the restaurant, including which food items to choose and the size of the portion. Promotional items are also useful to advertise the name of the restaurant.

Some promotional methods are used every day, for example the menu; other methods are used from time to time as a special effort to encourage custom, for example, discounts on a particular product.

The aims of all the promotional methods are:

- to increase sales by encouraging customers to buy more of the restaurant's products
- to increase customer satisfaction by making things attractive and making customers aware of all the items on offer
- to encourage customers to return to the restaurant.

An attractive display may result in *impulse buying*, the purchasing of food items on the spur-of-the-moment where there was no previous intention to buy.

Promotional methods

1. Staff selling Counter service staff deal directly with the customers, and are therefore in an ideal position to encourage sales.

Staff can promote sales by:	*For example:*
• being attentive to customers' needs	'You look as if you need warming up, Linda. Today's soup is delicious.'
• having a good knowledge of the food items offered on the menu, what ingredients are used in dishes, how they are cooked, and any changes to the menu	'The soup of the day is home made minestrone. There's parmesan cheese to go with it too.'
• being prepared to make suggestions to the customer, when appropriate	'Would you like a nice, high fibre, wholemeal roll with your soup?'
• enquiring whether the customer requires anything else	'Now, would you enjoy a slice of hot apple pie and custard to finish off your meal?'

2. Menus The menu itself promotes the products of the restaurant. Use of pictures, photographs and attractive descriptions can greatly encourage sales.

3. Displays The way that food is displayed on the counter can be used to encourage sales.

- The counter should be clean and tidy.
- The food items should be fresh (limp salads do not encourage customers to select them).
- The counter should appear full, but not overcrowded.

An attractive display will encourage food sales, while an untidy or poorly presented counter may actually discourage sales (see unit 9).

4. Positioning The position of the counters may be used to encourage sales, they should be located where they can easily be seen from the entrance to the restaurant. Lighting above the counter may be used to focus attention on the food and drink available.

5. Catering for children Some restaurants make a special effort to cater for children and families, providing high chairs, bibs and non-spill drinking cups. The menu often offers a choice of children's items consisting of smaller portions of items from the adult menu and sometimes additional children's favourites.

Puzzles and games may be provided to amuse children, and a play area may be set aside where parents can watch the children while they are eating.

6. Promotional material These are often called *point-of-sale promotions*. Chain restaurants often use the same promotional ideas at all their outlets.

- Logos: these are signs or symbols representing the name of the restaurant. Crockery, napkins, place mats, bills, and packaged items, such as sugar, may be used to promote the restaurant by having a 'logo' printed on them. Special events may also be promoted on these items.
- Posters: within the restaurant, the reception areas and the counters may be used to advertise special dishes or draw customers' attention to new products. Posters may be used to aid the customer in making a choice before reaching the counter, thus reducing the service time.
- Table cards: are placed on the tables where customers will eat the food to inform the customers of special dishes, offers and events. These must be replaced frequently in order that they do not become tatty.
- Table mats: the paper mats that are placed on the table or on the tray holding the customer's meal may be illustrated with a game or general knowledge information. The mats are often printed in sets of illustrations, encouraging customers to return to collect the rest of the set.
- Special events: some restaurants help organise special celebrations for occasions. These may be private events, such as children's birthday parties, or a special menu at Christmas or Easter. The restaurant may provide a host/hostess to entertain, and include games and presents for all the guests.
- Coupons: these are printed with some special offer to entice customers to return to the restaurant for a further visit, for example three meals for the price of two, or to try a particular product, such as a large size drink for the price of a small one.
- Premium gifts: these are gifts which are usually offered to children in the expectation that they will persuade their parents to take them to the restaurant to receive the gift. The gifts frequently include hats, games and toys. Large soft-drink glasses printed with cartoon characters are another popular premium gift. The items are usually printed with the restaurant name or 'logo'.
- Gift certificates or vouchers: these are used mostly by chain restaurants. The customers buy the certificates to give to friends and relatives, who can then receive without cost to themselves food and drink items up to the value of the certificate, from any one of the restaurant's outlets.

TO DO

Write down four ways in which a restaurant could promote the sale of coffee.

Attractive presentation of food is one of the most effective ways to encourage sales (see unit 8).

In most forms of counter service the food is on display for the customers to select their meal.

- Presentation of food and beverages shows customers what is on offer in a way that a printed menu cannot. They are able to select their meal knowing what it looks like.
- An attractive display will make the food look more appealing and encourage people to eat.
- Customers' satisfaction is increased when food is presented well, and customers who are satisfied are likely to return.
- This in turn may encourage them to recommend the restaurant to their friends.

All of which leads to increased sales and therefore higher profits.

Attractive presentation

1. Cleanliness Apart from the importance of keeping surfaces clean for reasons of hygiene (see unit 20), cleanliness is also important in producing an attractive and appetising display.

The counter surfaces should always be cleaned thoroughly before and after the service period. During service, spills and food debris should be cleared immediately.

2. Display equipment Although many food items have to be placed in the containers designed for the service counter (for example, Gastronorm containers), other foods, such as bread rolls and individually packaged sauces, can be attractively displayed in bowls and baskets. The food containers and display materials can be used to enhance the presentation of food and drink.

- Wicker baskets may be used to hold bread rolls or biscuits. These containers will make the food look far more appetising than a pile on a plate.
- Earthenware bowls can also be used to hold food.
- Displays of assorted fruit, such as apples, oranges, bananas and pears, may be placed at intervals along the counter. When more exotic fruits are in season these may also be used. Single pieces of fruit can add colour to otherwise uninteresting displays of food, for example a pineapple among plates of gâteaux.
- Wine bottles standing on their own or placed in wine baskets are also useful to add interest to a display.
- Doileys may be used to line containers and cover plates.
- Folded napkins may be used as decoration, or to line containers.

USEFUL TERM

Gastronorm containers Metal containers which fit into hotplates and bains-marie in the service counter, used to hold hot food. They are made to a standard international size.

3. Food arrangement Effective and attractive food presentation depends on the balance and arrangement of the food in the containers and on the plates.

The points to consider include:

- Colour —The imaginative use of colour on the counter can be very effective. Contrasting colours help to offset each other, for example, placing carrots between two trays of green vegetables.
- Shape —A variety of shapes will add interest, for example placing trays of filled rolls next to trays of sandwiches.
- Texture —This is not strictly a visual consideration, but good balance requires a variety, for example apple crumble next to rice pudding.
- Portion size—Match portion sizes and plates. An overcrowded plate looks messy and too large a plate makes the portion look mean (see unit 10).

Attractive presentation will also depend on the effectiveness of any decoration or garnishes which are used.

SERVICE TIP

Some food items may be presented on the counter with some of the cooking liquor to prevent them from drying out. Serving staff should ensure that when these items are served on to the customer's plate the liquid is drained. Examples of items which may need some of the liquid to retain freshness include steamed fish, and some vegetable dishes, such as garlic mushrooms.

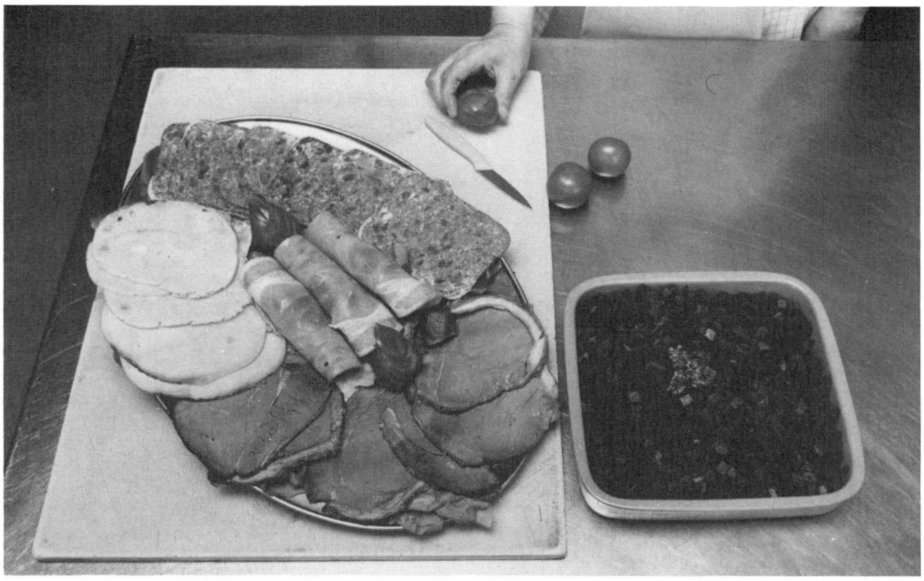

4. Garnishing A garnish is a decoration that is placed on a dish of food, usually once preparation or cooking has been completed. Garnishes may be cooked or uncooked. Cooked garnishes are usually served as accompaniments or side dishes.

Garnishes should be used to enhance the appeal of food items. They should be attractive, provide extra interest and be harmonious with the food served, in terms of colour, shape and flavour. Garnishes may include parsley, chopped egg yolk or egg white, diced red or green pepper, sliced lemon, stuffed olives, bacon rolls with roast turkey, pineapple rings with gammon steaks.

5. Information Customers like to be able to identify the foods they are eating and this is helped if they can see the foods clearly and recognise the dish. Cards with descriptions of the food and the nutritional content of each dish are useful. These may be folded tent cards placed in the appropriate place on the counter or cards fixed to the counter itself. The use of descriptive cards is particularly helpful for customers who are unable to eat some foods, for example vegetarians. Information cards may also include the price of the dish.

TO DO

Look closely at the presentation of food at your place of work, college restaurant or a restaurant of your choice. Make a list of the ways in which the presentation of the food could be improved.

The portions of the food and drink that are displayed and served from the counter should be of a standard size and composition. This is for two main reasons:

1. For the customers—who expect the portions to be the same size every time they visit the restaurant and not any more or less than other customers receive.
2. For the restaurant—the quantities of food and drink served to the customers must be controlled and standardised. Portions that are too large will lead to smaller profits for the restaurant while portions that are too small will lead to customer dissatisfaction and therefore loss of business.

To make sure that all portion sizes and all meals are standard, systems of *portion control* are used. In restaurants using counter service methods these are usually carried out by the service staff at the counter. Correct portioning can be achieved by a variety of means, but a basic requirement is that staff should be able to produce the correct portion size without difficulty.

*** FOR INTEREST**

Providing 1p worth of food over the standard portion per day in a restaurant that serves 1000 meals per day will cost £10 per day and lead to a loss of over £3000 per year.

Methods of portion control

Pre-portioning Many foods are sold in individual packs, the size of the portion being set by the manufacturer. Meat pies may be made in individual sizes; yoghurt is sold in individual cartons; accompaniments such as butter, sauces, salt and sugar are provided in individual packs.

Kitchen portioning Some foods may already have been portioned in the kitchen. Chicken legs, grilled chops and individual pies are examples of this. Items such as gâteaux and large cottage pies may have portion sizes clearly defined on them and the service staff have only to cut the item where indicated. Other items such as sliced meat, may be arranged on the dish in individual portions, each portion clearly separated.

Counter portioning There are two main methods of ensuring portion control for items that require portioning at the counter.

1. Providing equipment that serves the precise portion laid down, for example a soup ladle with a capacity of 200 ml (8 fl oz). Such equipment may be quite simple (a spoon or ladle), or quite sophisticated (a metred pump to dispense ice cream in precise quantities).

   Such equipment includes:

   - Ladles—variable sizes for serving soup, sauces, gravy and custard.
   - Scoops—for serving ice cream and mashed potato.
   - Spoons—of various sizes for serving portions of vegetables and similar foods.
   - Perforated spoons or wire scoops—for serving foods where excess liquid is not required, such as stews.

2. Serving the product in a container that holds a precise amount of the item, such as soup bowls, sweet bowls and glasses. In some restaurants these may be disposable cartons or cups. Less precisely, a size of plate or dish may be used that encourages portion control, for example, 23 cm (9 inch) diameter plates are often used to give the appearance of a plateful in carvery operations.

Portioning drinks

1. Sold in individual portions set by the manufacturer, the serving staff have only to pour the contents into a cup or glass.

2. Sold in bottles or containers which have marks to show each portion size.
3. Machine dispensed to give a standard portion, for example using optics to dispense spirits such as whisky and gin.
4. Dispensed by service staff into standard sized cups or glasses, which act as the measure for the portion, for example a pint mug for draught beer.

Different portion sizes may be available, such as *regular*, *large* and *extra large*.

TO DO

At your place of work or a restaurant of your choice, look at the ways in which the food and drink items are portioned. List a selection of 10 items showing how portion control is carried out for each item. Try and get examples as different as possible.

METHOD

Adequate preparation of the restaurant before opening is necessary to ensure that everything goes smoothly during the service period. The preparation tasks are usually carried out at the start of the day and then maintained by regular tidying and cleaning during quiet periods.

However in restaurants which are open throughout the day and night, sections of the counters and dining area are closed during quiet periods so that they can be cleaned, prepared and returned to service with the minimum of disruption.

In counter service restaurants there are two areas that need to be prepared: the counter and the dining area.

Cleaning

The counter

1. Clear the counter of display trays, containers, utensils, crockery, cutlery, service cloths and meal trays.
2. Switch off all equipment. Allow hot equipment to cool before cleaning.
3. Wear gloves and use disposable cloths.
4. Clean all surfaces, display cabinets, drinks dispenser and transparent screens with a detergent solution. Be careful to remove any grease and food debris trapped in corners.
5. Rinse all surfaces thoroughly with fresh, very hot water.
6. Food service containers and other small items such as ladles, scoops, tongs and spoons should be washed in a dish washer machine. If they have to be hand-washed, use a double or twin sink, one side filled with hot water at 60°C (140°F) and detergent in the correct solution and the other filled with very hot water at 80°C (180°F) in order to disinfect. Wire baskets should be used, as this is too hot for hands.
7. The detergent and rinsing water should be changed regularly.
8. Stubborn deposits should be removed with nylon brushes or nylon scouring pads. Steel wool or wire scouring pads should not be used as they will damage the surface of the equipment.
9. Pay particular attention to runners and sliding door channels. The shelves should be removed if possible (when the shelf supports also need to be cleaned).
10. All equipment must be thoroughly dried, preferably air-dried (serving equipment, crockery etc. on racks). Paper towelling is better than a linen cloth when air-drying is not possible.
11. Items must not be stacked for re-use unless they are absolutely dry.

The dining area

1. Suction-clean tiled or vinyl floors then mop with a detergent solution and allow to dry. Wet areas should be cordoned off for safety, and checked when dry for any soiling that remains.
2. Suction-clean carpeted areas.
3. Damp-dust all surfaces of tables and chairs including the legs, using a detergent solution. Remove any stains caused by spilt food and drink.
4. Collect the trays, wipe clean and stack at the appropriate place.
5. Empty rubbish bins and ash trays, clean and return to their correct places. Never empty ashtrays into bins which might set fire to themselves, or contain other rubbish which would burn.

Checking

The counter

1. Check crockery, cutlery and glassware for chips and cracks, and to ensure that it is clean. Also check all surfaces.
2. Refill the plate warmer and put piles of cold plates on the counter as necessary.

!! REMEMBER

Opening duties

- Make sure the dining room *temperature* is comfortable.
- Check the level of *lighting*; this will depend on the establishment. Check that all the light bulbs are working.
- Check *chair* and *table* positions.
- Check *pictures* and *posters* are hanging straight.
- Inspect the dining room and counter area for *cleanliness* and *safety*. Check the condition of the toilets.
- Make sure the *music* is organised and at the correct noise level.

3. Switch on all appliances to check that they are in good order. Report faults to the supervisor. Appliances that need time to attain the correct temperature, such as cold counters, hot cupboards and beverage dispensers, should be turned on in time to reach the required temperature before using.
4. Display the day's menu. Check menu board of standard items for any out of stock or new items, and for price changes.

The dining area

1. Report any uneven floor surfaces or frayed carpets to the supervisor.
2. Check that tables and chairs are in good condition and stable. Sit in chairs and feel under seats and table tops for damaged or sharp edges and discarded chewing gum.
3. Check that all lighting and ventilation systems are working and report any faults.
4. If menus are placed on the tables, check they are correct and not damaged or tatty looking.

Stocking

The counter

1. Place crockery, cutlery, glassware, napkins and trays at the appropriate places along the counter.
2. Bring cold food from the kitchen and arrange in the chilled cabinets. Hot food containers should be brought from the kitchen and placed on the counter immediately before service.

TO DO

Make your own detailed list of the preparation tasks that have to be carried out at your place of work or at a restaurant of your choice.

3. Place the correct serving equipment, such as ladles and spoons, by each of the food items.
4. Portion any starters or sweets (unless this has been done in the kitchen).
5. Check that there are plenty of back-up supplies of food items, crockery and cutlery to replenish during the serving period.
6. Arrange all food and beverage items so that customers can easily remove them from the cabinets without disturbing the presentation of the remaining items (see unit 9).

The dining area

1. Check and refill sauce bottles, mustard containers, salt and pepper pots or individual packets of items. Place on the tables or at the appropriate place by the counter.
2. Place promotional items, such as mats, on the tables.
3. Fill cutlery trays and napkin dispensers.

Cater Base

The information in this unit will help you gain the Caterbase modules: *Preparing the Counter for Counter Service* and *Preparing and Clearing the Dining Area for Counter Service.*

Buffet service

The amount of preparation required for buffet service will depend on:

- the type of buffet and the formality of the occasion
- whether part of the meal will be served by staff at the customers' tables
- whether the customers are to sit down at tables to eat the food.

Preparing the buffet table Many shapes of buffet tables can be used to display the food, depending on the space available and the number of customers who are to be served. Separate tables may be used to display separate courses, to increase the speed of flow and so that staff can clear dirty plates from a table as the meal proceeds.

1. *Table cloths*
The buffet table may need covering with a table cloth; this will:

- provide an attractive background for the food display
- hide an unsightly table top.

The cloth is usually fitted so that it reaches down to the floor at the sides the customers will see.

2. *Decoration*
For many buffets the food dishes are sufficiently attractive in themselves and no further decoration is necessary; however, sometimes flowers, ice carvings, butter mouldings and other features are used. These should be placed in position on the buffet table.

3. *Cutlery and crockery*
Hot and cold plates (as applicable) should be stacked at the head of each buffet table. Napkins and silverware are usually located at the end of the line unless the tables where the customers are to eat the food are laid.

Sufficient clean plates and cutlery should be available, so that the stack can be replenished throughout the service period.

4. *Food items*
The food items are brought to the buffet table just prior to the customers entering the dining area. Sufficient dishes should be brought to the buffet table so that the table looks fully laden, without resulting in dishes of food remaining on the table for long periods before they are required. Overcrowding should be avoided (see unit 8).

Preparing the customers' tables If the customers are to sit down to eat the food, the serving staff will be required to prepare the tables. Cutlery may be provided on the buffet table for the customers to take as required or the tables may be formally laid prior to service.

1. *Laying-up procedure*

- Assemble all the necessary cutlery and crockery, cleaned and polished.
- Place the cover plate (if used) 1.25 cm (½ inch) from the edge of the table, in a central position before each customer's chair. This makes it easier to lay the cutlery in the correct position.
- Lay the cutlery from the inside, so that cutlery which is to be used first during the meal lies on the outside of the place setting.
- Place the side plate to the left of the place setting.
- Place the side knife on the plate.
- Place the glass to the top right of the place setting, above the tip of the meat knife.
- Place a folded napkin on the cover plate, the side plate or in the glass according to the style of the restaurant.
- Place the cruet on the table.

✻ FOR INTEREST

Members of staff often work as a team, each person laying one item for the whole room or, alternatively, each person works alone, completing the tables he or she will be serving.

➧➧➧ TO DO

Make a list of all the items (cutlery, napkins, table cloths, crockery etc.) you would need to set the tables for a sit-down buffet for 50 people. The menu is as follows:

Minestrone soup
. . .
Selection of cold roast meats
Assorted salads
. . .
Selection of fruit flans and gâteaux
. . .
Coffee

USEFUL TERMS

Date stamp A date beyond which the product is past its best.
Shelf life The amount of time for which a product can be offered before it begins to deteriorate.

?? HOW TO

Clean a drinks vending machine

1. Collect all the items needed:
   - protective clothing
   - cleaning bucket, usually plastic for easy cleaning
   - cleaning cloths, paper or disposable if possible
   - nylon brushes to clean nozzles, tubes etc.
   - hand mops and sponges for interior and exterior cleaning
   - detergent and steriliser, non-toxic and taste free
   - exterior polish and cloths for cabinet cleaning.
2. Clean the parts that come into contact with the products:

   Daily
   - flush system with hot water from the machine.

   Twice weekly
   - Circulate cleaning solution through the system, leave for three minutes and flush several times with clean hot water.
   - Exchange mixing bowls, troughs and whippers for clean units and flush with hot water.
   - Flush and clean hoses with tube brushes and detergent. Flush with clean water.
3. Clean the other internal parts:
   - Work from the top downwards to avoid spillage on clean surfaces.
   - Wet-wipe all areas of spillage and splash. Dry-wipe all dust and powder spillage.
   - Clean all drainage areas, empty and clean waste container.
   - Clean inside of door, cup turret and cup chute.
   - Check for insect or vermin infestation.
4. Clean the exterior:
   - Wipe top, front and sides of machine.
   - Clean and disinfect the delivery area for the products.
   - Clean the area around the machine and ensure that the waste bin is empty.
   - Polish all exposed areas and metalwork.

2. *Completing the table*
Everything should be clean and laid symmetrically. For example, looking down the length of a long table all the glasses, cutlery and napkins should be in a straight line; on a round table they should all be laid the same distance from the centre.

For tables of two or four settings, place the cruet and flowers (if available) centrally. For tables of three use these items to balance the table but in a readily accessible position.

It is usual nowadays to keep clean ashtrays on the side and bring them to the tables when it is apparent that customers wish to smoke.

Vending service

The preparation of the machine on a daily basis is vital in order:

- to avoid health risks
- to provide a continuous service to the customer
- to keep the machine profitable for the operator.

1. *Cleaning*
Three areas need to be cleaned:

- the exterior and surroundings of the machine
- the general interior of the machine
- the parts that come into contact with food products.

2. *Restocking*

- Perishable items, such as sandwiches, need regular checking to ensure that deteriorating products do not remain in the machine, and to ensure that items do not run out.
- Items with a longer shelf life, such as wrapped sweets and snacks, will require frequent checking and refilling to ensure the items do not run out.
- Drinks—dry and liquid concentrate commodity canisters will need refilling. The dry canisters should be shaken to avoid caking. The supply of cups is vital to the operation and these should be regularly checked and replenished.

3. *Cash emptying*
Where cash is used to obtain items from the vending machine, regular emptying will be necessary to ensure the machine is working properly and for reasons of security.

13 METHOD

Some counter service situations require an order to be taken, in others there is no recorded order.

An order is necessary when:

- Serving staff are required to serve part of the meal at the customer's table, the customers helping themselves to other items from the counter. For example, carvery restaurants and steak houses which have a salad bar.
- Customers are served at the counter by the service staff.
- The customer's meal is made up in the kitchen to order, for example, in seated counter service.

No order is taken There are two main situations in which an order is not required:

- At counter service restaurants where the customers help themselves to food and drink items and take their selections to the till to pay for them.
- In restaurants where there is a set price for the meal, the customers help themselves to as much as they want from a buffet table.

Verbal orders Verbal orders are given by customers at the counter.

The staff may record the order on to an electronic cash register which will automatically calculate the bill, as in fast food service or the verbal order may simply be used to guide the staff as to the customer's needs, the customer taking the food to the till to pay.

!! REMEMBER

The serving staff should have a good knowledge of the menu and the food items offered, so that any customer queries can be answered. The serving staff should know:

- the ingredients of each dish, and how it has been prepared and cooked
- any additions or alterations to the menu
- if any items are unavailable.

Recording orders

Written order
A duplicate (making one extra copy of the order) or triplicate (making two extra copies of the order) check-pad is used. The pad may have a sheet of carbon paper between the copies or use self-carbonating paper.

—One copy goes to the kitchen, so that food can be prepared for the customer.
—One copy goes to the cashier, so that the food is charged for on the customer's bill.
—When a third copy is taken, it is usually kept by the serving staff for reference.

Computerised order
The order is taken mechanically, and processed electronically from the order terminal to the kitchen. The food items are automatically added to the customer's bill.

Points to note when taking orders:

- Make sure the customers are ready to order. If they are not, for example, if they are still studying the menu, return to take the order after a few minutes.
- Be helpful and attentive. Encourage sales by suggesting items that the customers might like.
- Write figures clearly on the order, in front of the name of the dish, thus

  2 Prawn Cocktails

- If carbon paper is used in the check-pad, make sure it is correctly placed.
- Draw a line between the orders for different courses.
- Use the same name for the dish as that used on the menu.
- Make a note of any special requirements, for example, how a steak should be cooked.
- Read back the order to the customers to ensure it has been taken correctly.

!! REMEMBER

Information required on the order

- Date
- Server's initials or code number
- Details of the order, clearly written.

In some restaurants the service staff may also need to record the table number and the number of customers to be served.

TO DO

Find among your local restaurants, fast-food shops and take-aways at least three examples of different ordering systems. Try and find out how well they work, and make your own notes on the advantages and disadvantages for each. Would you recommend that any of those sampled should change their system. If so write a brief report explaining why.

14 METHOD

Serving staff are required to serve some food and beverage items to customers in counter service restaurants where the food items are not pre-packed or pre-plated.

General points

Temperature of the plates

The plates should be at the correct temperature, *hot* food must be served on *hot* plates, *cold* food on *cold* plates.

Hygiene

Care should be taken not to touch the food on the plates. Items should always be served with a serving implement, serving staff should not use fingers to place items on the plates.

Highly perishable foods such as cream cakes should be displayed for as short a time as possible and uneaten items should be disposed of. Unless items are packaged and marked with a date stamp to indicate that they will keep, no food items should be offered on the following day.

Position of the food on the plates

- If the plate has a name or crest printed on it, this should be at the top of the plate when it is presented to the customer, in a 12 o'clock position. Customers should be able to read the name or see the crest properly without having to turn their heads (or rotate the plates).
- The main food item (meat, fish or eggs etc.) should be placed at the bottom of the plate, in a 6 o'clock position when it is presented to the customer.
- Portions of the sweet, which are triangular in shape should be placed with the point facing towards the customer.

Display

Some food items are placed on the counter in the cooking sauce to keep the item moist until it is served. When the liquid is not part of the dish to be eaten, the item should be drained carefully, before it is placed on the customer's plate. For example mushrooms à la grêcque and marinated herrings. Boiled or steamed vegetables should never be left standing in the cooking water. This will destroy their nutritional value.

Certain food items may only be displayed for a certain length of time, before looking unappetising and becoming inedible, for example, sauces may form a skin if they are not used quickly.

Points to note when serving

1. Serving staff should take care to hold hot plates with a cloth and warn customers when the plates are very hot.
2. Care should be taken that sauce or gravy is not spilt on to the rim of the plate. If this happens the rim should be wiped with a clean serving cloth.
3. The correct utensil should be used to serve each food item (see unit 10). A clean serving utensil should be used for each dish.
4. The main part of the meal, for example meat or fish, should be served first, then the potatoes and finally the vegetables.
5. Do not pile items on top of one another. The exception to this rule is where rice or pasta are part of the meal, and the sauce is placed on top of the rice or pasta.
6. Enquire where the customer would like the sauce or gravy, for example, beside the meat or poured over it.
7. While serving foods, place the container lids to one side or below the counter to enable customers to see the dishes. Replace lids during quiet periods to keep the food hot.
8. It is important that foods that were prepared first are served first. A strict rotation of food containers should be maintained.

Using a serving spoon and fork Although it is easier to serve some items such as small boiled potatoes and peas using only a spoon, it is useful at times to use a spoon and fork held in one hand to serve food items.

- The curve of the fork should lie in the bowl of the spoon.
- Hold the two together so that the palm of the hand and all the fingers are over both handles.
- Make sure the two are comfortably balanced.
- Insert the first finger midway between the spoon and fork handles. This acts as a lever so that the fork prongs and spoon bowl may be opened and closed to hold the items securely.

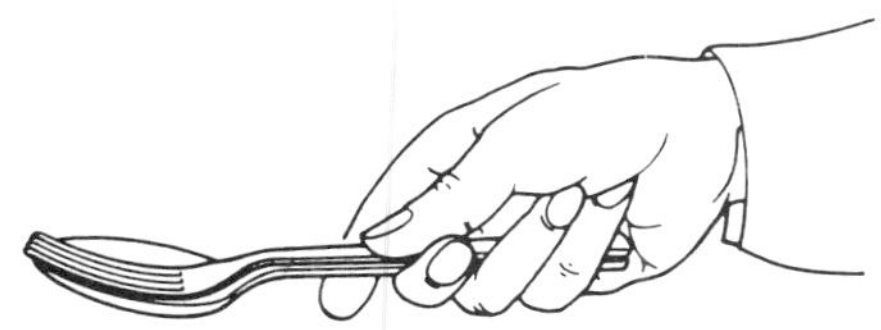

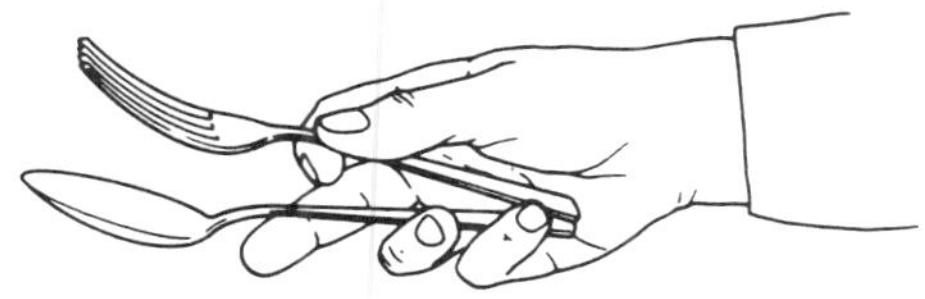

Carving Roast joints may require carving at the buffet table and this is usually done by a skilled server. Carving needs preparation and practice:

1. Knives should be very sharp.
2. Always carve against the grain of the meat, except for saddles of lamb.
3. Smoked salmon is carved very thinly. Ham, pork and beef are sliced thinly. Lamb, mutton and veal are sliced a little more thickly.

SERVICE TIPS

Certain foods may be served using two service forks or two fish knives, for example, omelettes, but this depends on the policy of the restaurant.

It may be easier to use the fork, prongs downwards, for example, when serving grilled tomatoes.

When serving dishes with a pastry crust, the crust should be portioned and placed to one side, the filling spooned on to the plate and the crust placed on top of the filling.

TO DO

Practise using a spoon and fork to serve food, either at home or at work during a free moment. Arrange a selection of different shaped items on a serving dish (the items need not be cooked food, but could be raw food, for example, new potatoes).

15 METHOD

In counter service restaurants, beverages may be served by the serving staff or the customers may serve themselves from vending machines on the counter. Cans, bottles and pre-served glasses of cold drinks may be placed in a chilled cabinet for customers to select.

Ways of serving hot beverages

- Poured out in a cup — from a large pot brewed by the staff
  — from a vending machine behind the counter
  — using individual tea and coffee bags, or instant coffee, with boiling water from an urn.
- In an individual pot made to order for each customer. Usually a tea or coffee bag is used, with boiling water from an urn. Some restaurants may provide a separate pot of hot water.

!! REMEMBER

- If the beverage is made in a large pot and poured as the customer requests it, care should be taken that the brew of tea and coffee does not stand for too long. Throw away old brews.
- When the milk or cream is served by the counter staff, the customers should be asked whether they require it. In many counter service restaurants the milk and cream are individually portioned for customers to take as they require.
- Be careful not to spill drinks into the saucer, if this occurs, a clean saucer should be provided. Do not overfill the cup, it will be difficult to carry.
- When a machine is used to dispense drinks, it is vital to switch it on in advance of the service period to ensure that the drinks are served at the correct temperature, hot drinks served hot and cold drinks served cold.

Making a pot of tea

1. Pre-heat the teapot with very hot water and empty away before adding the tea. This means that the water is at boiling point when it comes into contact with the tea, in order to extract the full strength and flavour.
2. Use the correct amount of tea or the correct size of tea bag for the teapot used.

Pot for 1	— one teaspoon and one for the pot
Pot for 2	— two teaspoons and one for the pot
$2\frac{1}{4}$ litres ($\frac{1}{2}$ gallon) pot	— about 22 grams ($\frac{3}{4}$ oz)
$4\frac{1}{2}$ litres (1 gallon) pot	— about 36 grams ($1\frac{1}{4}$ oz)

3. When the water, which should be freshly drawn, is boiling fiercely, pour it immediately into the heated pot. Bring the pot to the kettle, not the kettle to the pot.
4. Let the tea infuse for 5 minutes. Stir the pot. When a 10 or 20 litre multipot is used, it should be allowed to infuse for 15 minutes before pouring.
5. Milk and sugar—half a litre (1 pint) of milk should be enough for 26 normal sized cups of tea. Ask if the customer would like sugar, where the serving staff are required to serve sugar at the counter. If lemon slices are available, these should be offered as an alternative to milk with tea.

Making coffee

1. *Instant*
Instant coffee may be made in the cup, using either an individually wrapped sachet or a teaspoonful from a jar.

- Place one slightly heaped teaspoonful in the cup.
- Pour on boiling water.
- Stir to dissolve the coffee.
- Add hot or cold milk to the customer's taste.

2. *Coffee bags*
Ground coffee is sealed in bags that are designed to make either one cup of coffee or a quantity such as one litre or four litres. The method is similar to that used to make tea.

3. *Expresso*
Boiling water is forced through a condenser into ground coffee.

- Check temperature and pressure gauge of the machine.
- Add ground coffee to the filter, one dessert-spoonful of coffee per cup makes average strength coffee.
- Press down the grounds into the filter.
- Insert the filter into the machine.
- Press button to start steam infusion.
- Serve.

4. *Vacuum pot or cona*
These percolators use the principle of convection to send boiling water up to infuse a container of coffee above.

- Measure cold water into lower bowl and heat.
- Place appropriate amount of ground coffee (one dessert-spoonful per cup) into top bowl, insert this into the lower bowl when the water boils.
- Once most of the water has risen, stir gently and leave for 2 minutes on low heat.
- Turn off heat and allow coffee to filter down.
- Remove top bowl and serve.

5. *Filter equipment*
Melitta filters and equipment are among those used in Britain. A filter funnel, in which the coffee is placed, fits on top of the pot, glass or cup through which the coffee slowly percolates.

- Measure the coffee into a fresh filter paper in the holder.
- Add a little very hot water—about 95°C (200°F)—to moisten the coffee, wait 1 minute.
- Add the full quantity of water (at the same temperature, just below boiling point—if it is any hotter the flavour of the coffee may be spoilt) and allow to filter. Pour the water in a circular movement so it flows through all the coffee evenly.
- Remove filter and serve.

With electric filter machines, follow the manufacturer's instructions.
Coffee may be served black, with hot or cold milk or with cream.

?? HOW TO

Re-stock a drinks vending machine

1. Open the front of the machine.
2. Load the cups from a sealed carton into the cup turrets, ensuring that all turrets are full. Do not touch the rims of the cups.
3. Remove and shake the dry commodity canisters to prevent caking of the powder. Check the level of the products: tea, coffee, chocolate and soup. Refill with the manufacturer's recommended product to the maximum indicated level.
4. Check liquid concentrate canister and replace if nearly empty.
5. Replace all containers in their correct positions and after cleaning (see unit 12), vend one of each product to check operation and quality.
6. Close up machine and return all restock items to storage area.

➧➧➧ TO DO

On the next few occasions you have tea or coffee in a self-service restaurant, note how it is made, what equipment is used and how you found the product. If possible speak to the staff to learn what they think of the equipment.

Cater Base

The information in this unit will help you gain the Caterbase module *Serving and Clearing of Food and Beverages in Counter Service.*

Clearing the dining area

There are three methods used to clear the dining area of dirty plates and cutlery in counter service restaurants.

1. Customer clearing—the customers clear their own dirty crockery and rubbish once they have finished their meal.
2. Trolley clearing—the tables are cleared by the service staff after the customers have finished the whole meal and have left the tables. Trolleys are used to collect the dirty items.

3. Clearing at the table—the table is cleared by the serving staff, the dirty items are taken directly to the wash-up area or are collected on a tray before being removed from the dining area.

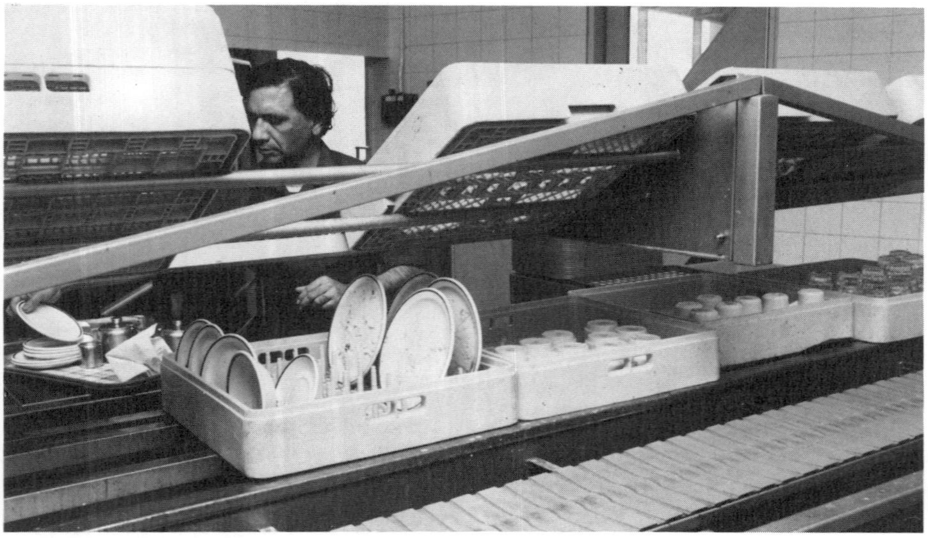

Customer clearing

- Where disposable plates and cutlery are used the customers take their trays to the appropriate area, place the plates, cups and cutlery in a bin and stack the trays on a shelf beside it.
- The customers take the trays to a clearing area, dispose of the rubbish in a bin, and stack the crockery and trays beside it.
- Conveyor belts may be used to take the dirty items to the wash-up area, the customers simply place their trays on the conveyor belt, and the trays are unloaded away from the dining area by the serving staff.

?? HOW TO
Clear plates

To remove plates with cutlery, pick up the plates with the right hand (if right handed) and stack them on the left hand.

1. Take a firm hold of the plate with the thumb over the rim and the first two fingers under it.
2. Transfer the plate to the other hand, with the thumb over the rim and the first two fingers under it. The third and fourth fingers should be crooked upwards to receive the second plate.
3. With the free hand scrape any remaining food into a pile.
4. Arrange the knife and fork at right angles with the knife blade under the bridge of the fork.
5. Pick up the second customer's plate, place it on the forearm, supported by the third and fourth fingers.
6. Scrape any remaining food on to the first plate, and place the knife and fork with the other cutlery.
7. Continue to clear plates, stacking them on the forearm.

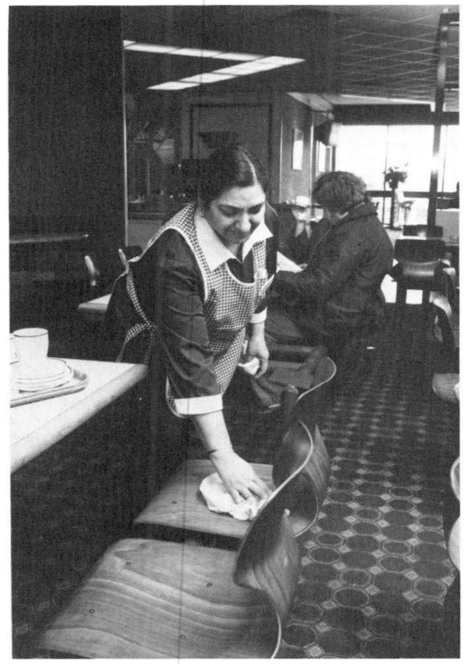

In all customer clearing situations there is still a need for staff to help with the clearing. Some customers forget or do not bother to clear, the bins need emptying, the clearing areas will need frequent clearing and cleaning and the dining tables will need wiping. Rubbish bins must be emptied frequently and kept spotlessly clean, including the area around the bin where spillages may occur. The floor of the dining area will need regular sweeping, especially under the dining tables.

This method of clearing is used in cafeteria style restaurants, for example in colleges, department stores and fast food restaurants.

Trolley clearing When the customers have finished eating and left the table, it is cleared by serving staff using a clearing trolley.

- The trolley is wheeled to the table.
- The crockery and glasses are stacked and the cutlery placed in a cutlery tray on the trolley.
- Rubbish is placed in a bin, which is either positioned on a platform at one end of the trolley or hangs from a bar.
- The table and seats are wiped with a clean cloth.
- The floor area under and around the table should be swept and any rubbish or spills cleaned up.

Trolley clearing was popular in large staff dining rooms and department store restaurants, but many establishments have changed to tray clearing at the table.

Clearing at the table

- Clearing should commence when all the customers at the table have finished eating.
- Clearing should be carried out systematically around the table, in such a way that no customer feels forgotten.
- Clearing should be carried out as quietly as possible.

This method is used in more and more counter service situations, especially where part of the meal is served to the customers at the table, for example carveries, buffets and seated counter service, and in motorway service restaurants.

Clearing the counter

Regular cleaning and tidying of the counter area should take place during the service period, but there will still be times when the area needs thorough cleaning. This may take place once the meal session has finished or in restaurants that are open 24 hours a day will take place during quiet periods when sections of the counter may be closed.

- Containers that are full or partly full should be returned to the kitchen where the contents can be dealt with appropriately.
- Packaged and non-perishable items such as pots of jam should be returned to the correct storage area.
- Empty food containers and food service equipment should be sent to the wash-up area.
- Rubbish should be carefully disposed of in the correct bins.
- All power supplies to the counter equipment should be switched off.
- All surfaces should be thoroughly cleaned before restocking takes place.

Buffet service

During service empty, or nearly empty, serving dishes will need to be removed from the buffet table. Where separate tables are used to display different courses, the tables can be cleared once the customers have finished eating the course. Decorative dishes are usually left on the tables until the meal is completed.

At the end of the meal, once the customers have left the dining area, all the tables should be cleared.

TO DO

Practise clearing the dinner table at home:

(a) when the family or your friends are at table (for example, after the main course)—do this without the help of a tray

(b) when everyone has left the table, when you should use a tray—see how neatly you can stack the tray without making the whole process take too long.

17

The way that customers pay for their meal varies according to the way that the order for the food and beverages was taken.

Verbal orders

- In self-service restaurants, payment is made to a cashier located at the end of the counter. Customers take their selected items to the cashier and pay before eating the items.
- In fast food restaurants, orders are given verbally, recorded in the till and payment is taken by the serving staff before the customer receives the items.

Written orders

- In some counter service restaurants, such as carveries and buffets, the order is written and a copy goes to the cashier. At the end of the meal the orders for the table are totalled and the total bill is presented to the customer who may pay at the table or at the cash desk.
- In seated counter service, the customer is given a copy of the order with the prices included. When the customer has finished, the serving staff totals the bill from the orders and takes payment.

Example 1

```
Quick Burger
High St
Townsville
(2)
VAT No 12345        1/1/99—(1)

4 large
  cheeseburgers  8.00
2 portions chips 1.00
2 coffees         .90
2 coca colas     1.20

           Total 11.10—(4)
```

Preparing the bill

Three methods are found in counter service establishments:

1. Direct entry into an automatic cash register—the serving staff enter the items ordered and the prices are recorded in the machine which automatically totals the items. This method is often found in fast food restaurants.
2. A cashier enters the prices for the items into a cash register, which automatically totals the bill.
3. The serving staff or cashier total the bill from the written order checks. This system is likely to be found only in buffet service. When the bill has been prepared it should be presented for payment—either when the customer requests it or at the end of the meal after the coffee has been served. The bill is folded in half on a plate, so that only the person who is paying sees the total, and taken to the table. The serving staff should leave the customer to check the details and place the payment on the plate, returning to sort out any queries and to take the payment.

!! REMEMBER

Cheque checkpoints

Check the cheque:

- Is the *date* correct?
- Does the *amount* in words and figures agree?
- Does the signature match that on the card?
- Was the cheque signed in front of you?

Check the cheque card:

- Has the card expired?
- Does the signature match the one on the cheque?
- Does the code number match the one on the cheque?

Taking payment

1. Cash

- Count the money carefully in front of the customer.
- Enter the amount that the customer has given into the till.
- Most tills automatically record the amount of change to be given.
- Take the amount of change from the till and count it carefully for the customer.

2. Cheque

- Make sure the cheque is filled out correctly, and that a valid cheque card is supporting the cheque.
- Amounts over £50 or in some cases £100 will require other identification, such as a current driving licence or a passport.
- Write the cheque card number on the back of the cheque.

?? HOW TO

Give change

For example, if the bill is £2.40 and the customer gives a £5 note, take two £1 coins from the till and three 20p coins, and count the money into the customer's hand. It is usually helpful to count up from the amount the bill comes to, to the amount tendered. In this example:

1. 'Two pounds forty pence.'
2. 'Two pounds sixty pence'
   Hand over 1st 20p coin
3. 'Two pounds eighty pence'
   Hand over 2nd 20p coin
4. 'Three pounds'
   Hand over 3rd 20p coin
5. 'Four pounds'
   Hand over 1st £1 coin
6. 'Five pounds, your change sir/madam, thank you'.
   Hand over 2nd £1 coin

Example 2

```
The Carvery
Riverside  ②
VAT No 456789                10/11/99—①

2 buffet lunches @ £8.95      17.90
1 bottle wine No 33            6.95

           Sub total          24.85
           Service @ 12%       2.98—③

           Total              27.83—④
```

① Date—date on which meal is eaten.
② Name and address of the restaurant—together with the VAT registration number, if applicable. This is usually pre-printed on the bill.
③ Service charge—some restaurants add a set percentage as a service charge, others leave it to the customers to tip staff as they feel fit.
④ Total—this is the total amount to be paid, including VAT and any service or cover charge.

3. Credit card Some customers in department stores and motorway service area restaurants will pay by credit card, for example, Access, Barclaycard, American Express, or the store's or company's own charge card.

- Check that the particular card is acceptable, and check the details on the card carefully:
  —Has the card expired?
  —Is the card on a list of lost or stolen cards?
- Put the card through the electronic imprinter and enter the details of the charge. If a hand-operated imprinter is in use, put the card and the voucher through together, then fill in the other details by hand:
  —date
  —description of goods sold, for example 'Food'
  —amount
  —your initials
  —authorisation code (if the amount is over the 'floor' limit).
- Present the voucher for signature.
- Check that the signature matches the one on the card.
- Give the appropriate copy of the voucher to the customer, with the credit card and receipt.
- Place the other copies in a secure place, usually in the till.

4. Other methods of payment

- Regular customers, at buffets for example, may have an account at the restaurant.
- Foreign currency is accepted in some establishments, for example airport self-service restaurants.
- Token systems are used in some staff restaurants. The tokens may be issued to staff with their wage envelopes, or sold to them by someone in the accounts or personnel department. They are exchanged for food and drinks at the restaurant. This avoids the need for food serving staff to handle cash.
- Cards are also used in staff canteens. The cards have a set value recorded electronically on them, working in the same way as Phonecards. The cost of the meal is deducted from the card by inserting it into a machine. Some cards operate meal vending machines (see unit 7).
- Luncheon vouchers are given by some companies to their staff to spend on food and drink as they wish—either in the staff restaurant or in pubs, snack bars and in other establishments outside the premises, even supermarkets.

USEFUL TERMS

Bill Totalled list of charges relating to food and drinks consumed.
VAT Value Added Tax charged on many goods and services, paid to the government.
Float A sum of money (mostly coins but with some £5 notes) which is placed in the till at the start of service so that change can be given to customers. At the end of service the float is removed for safe-keeping (and exchanged, if necessary for more small change), leaving the takings.

TO DO

On the next few occasions you go shopping, make a point of noting how the payment is dealt with:

- the good points, for example saying 'thank you' pleasantly, counting the change back properly, adding up quickly and accurately
- and the bad, for example not speaking at all, throwing the change down on the counter in a handful of coins, trying to slip in foreign coins.

If you are working at a cash desk in the future, try and learn from the good points and avoid the bad.

Cater Base

The information in this unit will help you gain the Caterbase module *Taking Payment for Counter Service*.

18 CUSTOMERCRAFT

Serving involves close contact with customers and food and means that individual staff members are under constant and close observation. It is therefore important for staff to maintain high standards of personal presentation, including personal hygiene and dress.

!! REMEMBER

- Never lick the fingers.
- Keep hands really clean.
- Never touch the hair.
- Protect cuts and grazes with a clean dressing.
- Avoid using a handkerchief in the serving area.
- Do not eat, drink or chew while on duty.
- Do not smoke on duty.
- Never touch food on the plates.
- Never hold clean plates, cups, glasses or cutlery at those points where contact with food, drink or the customer's mouth will occur.
- If you are suffering from any medical conditions let your supervisor know.

Personal hygiene

1. *Fingernails and hands*
These are always on show. It is vital to wash hands immediately before service and after using the toilet. Nails should be trimmed and kept clean. Although many establishments do not insist, it is preferable to avoid nail polish. Smokers should take special care that their hands are clean.

2. *Bodily cleanliness*
Any odour will be offensive to customers, frequent bathing is important. Scent, perfume, cologne or aftershave should be avoided.

3. *Hair*
This should be kept clean, well groomed and away from the face. It should also be kept away from the food: covered with a hat or cap, long hair tied back.

4. *Mouth*
Clean teeth and breath are important as serving staff are often in close proximity to customers and do not want to cause offence.

5. *Feet*
Feet need care for comfort and hygiene. Toe nails should be trimmed frequently.

6. *Ill health*
When a member of staff has a cold or is feeling unwell, it is better for him or her to stay away from work, than to risk infecting other staff members or customers. Germs can be transmitted quickly when handling food.

SERVICE TIP

Wearing a lot of *jewellery* should be avoided: it will get in the way when serving, will distract customers and may be unhygienic.

Clothing

Whether a uniform is provided by the restaurant, or serving staff are expected to wear their own clothes, clothing worn for serving should:

- be comfortable and practical
- allow for free movement
- be hygienic
- look good to the customers and the members of staff
- blend with the atmosphere of the restaurant
- have strong pockets to hold note pads, cork screws etc.

A change of work clothes is necessary to allow for laundering. Daily washing of washable clothing is desirable.

Shoes

Serving staff spend the major part of their working hours on their feet, so comfortable, practical shoes are a priority. It is important that shoes have a non-slip sole and heels are of a practical height. Open-toed shoes should not be worn. In the event of an accident a sturdy pair of shoes will protect the feet from hot liquids and dropped plates. Shoes should be kept clean and in good repair.

Attitudes, behaviour and verbal skills

In counter service, staff have very little time to spend with any one customer, therefore it is important to make good use of the time available to create the right impression.

The customer's perception of the quality of service will be influenced by the attitude of the serving staff, their behaviour and what they say.

Four skills are important.

1. Attentiveness to customer needs This means observing what a customer wants and providing for that need—treating people as individuals not just bodies in a queue.

Certain needs can be observed from the type of customer, for example:

Children	may need high chairs and smaller portions.
Elderly people	may need help with reading the menu, carrying the food to the table and clearing their plates after the meal.
Customers in wheelchairs	may need to be served at the table. They also may require help in finding a table with space for the chair.

Other needs may be established by observing the customers' behaviour or body language, and listening to what they say and how they say it:

Behaviour and body language	Customers may give non-verbal signs that they are impatient, by folding their arms as they stand in the queue, or, dissatisfied with the choice on the counter, by peering at one dish after another, lifting them up then banging them down.
Listening to what the customer says	Pay attention to the customer who is being served. If a customer has difficulty with the language show patience and understanding.
Listen to how the customer says it	Listen, not only to what a customer is saying, but how it is said. This can say a lot about whether a customer is annoyed.

In helping customers to feel relaxed and comfortable, the serving staff show they have their interest at heart.

2. Empathy and rapport The serving staff should be able to place themselves in the customer's position, and understand how they would feel if they were the customer.

3. Using the right body language

- A *smile* will immediately create a friendly welcoming impression.
- *Eye contact* implies interest.
- Slouched posture, for example leaning on the counter, gives a bad impression; a deliberate upright posture implies confidence and enthusiasm.

4. Using the right words at the right time The ability to say, in the right way, the right thing at the right time is the essence of communication and very important in providing for customers' needs.

Servers' tact in handling a problem, a respectful 'sir' and 'madam' when talking to customers, their knowledge of the food items, and the help they provide, are vital in contributing to a pleasant experience.

?? HOW TO

Deal with complaints

Any complaint about the service or food should be dealt with immediately, with an apology. If the complaint is about an item of food, the serving staff should:

- Apologise to the customer.
- Ask if another serving of the same dish is required or an alternative.
- Serve the new dish as soon as possible.
- Apologise for the inconvenience.

If there has been a complaint, it is important to ensure that warm and friendly relations have been re-established before the customers leave the restaurant and that they feel that they will be welcomed on a return visit.

TO DO

Start making a list of what pleases you about the way staff serve you in shops, banks, restaurants etc. Divide your list up into five columns and when you note a point, consider whether it is to do with:

(a) their *appearance*
(b) how *helpful* they are in attending to your needs
(c) the way they use *body language* to give you the best impression as well as to notice how you are reacting
(d) what *they say*
(e) their *knowledge* of their job

and enter it in the appropriate column.

MASTERCRAFT

See Customercraft book and video, *Servicecraft Food and Beverage Service*, and video *Servicecraft 2: Counter Service*

19 WORKING METHODS

In order to provide customers with the standard of service they expect it is important that counter service staff are efficient in their methods of working. Serving staff who are punctual, helpful, and aware of the needs of the customers will greatly contribute to the smooth running of the restaurant and the customers' enjoyment of the meal.

Working as a team

Each member of the serving staff is dependent on others for the successful completion of tasks. The organisation of the staff team will depend on the size and type of unit. A small take-away shop, for example, may only have a staff of two carrying out all the necessary duties, from cooking the food to taking the payment. Large canteens may employ 100 staff, each of whom is responsible for a different task.

- Be willing to help colleagues and managers.
- Try to be pleasant at all times and maintain a good relationship with other members of staff.
- Be prepared to share equipment and materials, more than one member of staff may wish to use a piece of equipment at one time. Getting angry with colleagues will not serve the customers more quickly.

Timing

One of the most valuable skills to be learnt in food service is that of organising the tasks to be carried out during the service period, so that the serving procedure at the counter runs smoothly, and that the customers do not have to queue for any longer than necessary.

Counter serving staff should:

- Be able to estimate the time it will take to prepare the counter for service, to serve the food and for customers to collect and pay for it. It is also helpful to be able to predict how long customers will take to eat their meals, especially if it is busy and the tables must be cleared as soon as they leave.
- Be familiar with food preparation times, so that customers can be informed of any likely delays and so that the kitchen can be informed in time if it is necessary to prepare more food.
- Be aware of rush periods (for example, between 12 and 2 o'clock in the works canteen, or after the pubs have closed in the fish and chip shop) and ensure they have sufficient prepared food on the counter to cope.
- Keep an eye on the counter at all times, restocking items where necessary. The kitchen should be alerted that replenishment is necessary before a dish is completely finished on the counter.

Punctuality Serving staff have a responsibility, both to other members of staff and the customers, to be punctual. If members of staff turn up late for duty other staff members will have to cover for them, causing delay and resentment.

Coping with pressure When the restaurant is very busy, long queues may form at the counter and customers may be required to wait for some time before obtaining their food. Panicking will not achieve faster or more efficient service.

Advise customers how long they may have to queue and ensure that service is carried out at the counter as quickly as possible.

!! REMEMBER

- Inform customers if there is going to be a delay in serving any item.
- Ensure that sufficient clean trays, plates and cutlery are available throughout the service period.
- Make sure that when customers are clearing their own tables the dirty crockery is not left for long in the dining area before being removed for washing.

Avoiding wastage

Working efficiently includes avoiding wastage. Serving staff should:

- Ensure that all appliances are turned off when not in use in order to save gas and electricity.

- Ensure that, while meanness is avoided, there is no unnecessary waste of food.
- Make sure that no more food is displayed than is likely to be eaten at one meal session, ensure back-up supplies are necessary if requested.

Catering for customers with special needs

Serving staff may be required to cater for blind or disabled people, the aim being to maintain as normal a service as possible, while paying consideration to the needs of the customers.

Some customers may need more help in obtaining their meals, and in finding seating than others.

1. Elderly people
   - There must be easy access to their table.
   - An upright chair may be required.
2. Blind customers
   - There must be easy access to their table.
   - They should be placed at a table where they will not have to move for other customers.
3. Deaf customers
   - They should be placed where they can see everything.
   - They should be placed where there are even noise levels, away from the stereo or telephone.
   - Listen, carefully to the customer's voice, it may not be very clear.
4. Customers in wheelchairs
   - Easy access to the table is essential.
5. Catering for children
   - Give the child a high chair or cushion to sit on.
   - Place the child where it is possible to see what is going on.
   - Seat the family where noise will cause the least disturbance to other customers.

TO DO

An important part of working as a team is knowing what your colleagues do, and their responsibilities. With this information you are also likely to be able to give customers more help, because you know who will have the answer you don't have.

Make a list of the names of all your colleagues, with a short description of what they look like and notes on their job. If you are not working at present, look back on your last job and try and do the same exercise.

20 WORKING METHODS

Serving staff have a responsibility to ensure that safe and hygienic standards are maintained in the restaurant and the serving areas.

Safety in counter service

Safety means preventing accidents that can harm staff or customers. Serving staff can help to prevent accidents by:

1. Observing and following closely all required work procedures, for example by properly completing cleaning tasks.
2. Keeping the work areas in a safe condition, for example by removing all used plates to the wash-up area as soon as possible, rather than letting dirty crockery and equipment pile up on the tables and behind the counter.
3. Keeping the floors clean and dry, both on the customer's side of the counter and behind the counter itself, and clearing up dropped food immediately.
4. Reporting any problems requiring repair and maintenance as soon as they are observed, for example a damaged table or a loose tile on the floor.
5. Notifying supervisors immediately of any accident, however slight.

Hygiene in counter service

The serving staff's responsibility for hygiene does not end with their own personal hygiene (see unit 18), nor does the need for proper sanitary procedures end once the food has been prepared.

At many industrial catering units a sample is taken each day of each dish. The samples are dated and then stored in a refrigerator for 3 to 5 days. In this way, if there is a suspected case of food poisoning the source can be accurately traced.

In counter service restaurants special care must be taken as customers may touch or breath over food before making a selection. In some situations it is possible to prevent this by:

- providing 'sneeze screens', transparent screens covering the food display which may be opened from the customers' side of the counter
- covering plated food items and snacks with plastic film
- providing adequate serving utensils for customers to serve food items without using their fingers.

Other hygienic procedures
These include:

- covering food before and during service—this avoids contamination by dust, insects and from sneezing or coughing

?? HOW TO
Prevent common accidents

Burns and scalds
- Treat hotplates and warming dishes carefully to avoid burns.
- Warn customers when plates are very hot.
- Keep handles turned away from busy areas.
- Use dry cloths to hold hot plates.
- Take care with candles on buffet tables.

Falls
- Keep floor areas clean and dry.
- Remove all hazards from the floor, for example dirty linen, dropped food.
- Open and shut doors carefully.
- Walk, don't run.
- Wear sensible shoes while on duty.
- Don't leave cables for electrical equipment lying dangerously across floors.

Cuts
- Take care when using knives.
- Keep sharp articles away from serving areas.
- Load trays and trolleys so dishes will not slide off.
- Clear up broken glass or china immediately.

Take special care when using electrical equipment—ensure that hands are dry, and switch off and unplug the equipment when it is not in use.

- keeping cold food refrigerated before and during service
- avoiding using hotplates to heat food—they should only be used to keep hot food hot
- not ordering too much food at a time, so that it has to stand around on the counter for a long time
- cleaning up any spilt food as soon as the spill occurs
- using separate serving utensils for different food items
- always holding cutlery by the handle and not touching the eating surface
- always holding crockery by the rim
- always holding glasses by the stem or base
- never serving food that has been displayed the previous day
- practising sanitary personal habits—serving staff should not smoke, eat, chew, sneeze, cough or otherwise practise bad habits in the serving, dining or kitchen areas (see unit 18).

Unavoidable accidents Even when all obvious precautions have been taken, an accident may still occur. It is therefore important for staff to know what to do in the case of an accident.

Knowledge of first aid—immediately after an accident has occurred, first aid is the primary concern. In most establishments one of the staff members will be properly trained. A first aid kit should be available in the serving area or kitchen and all members of the staff should be aware of where it is kept. If information on the basic treatment of common accidents, such as burns and scalds, is displayed, become familiar with it.

Fire—serving staff should know where fire-extinguishing equipment is located and how to use it. In large establishments fire drills will ensure that staff are aware of exits and are sure of their roles in aiding customers to leave the premises. Staff working in small units should sort out an action routine in the event of a fire.

Any accident should be reported to the supervisor immediately. A clear statement of the events leading to the accident should be recorded, usually on special forms or in the accident book.

!! REMEMBER

- Any cleaning tasks which are the responsibility of the serving staff should be thoroughly carried out, both from the point of hygiene and of safety.
- Floor areas should be kept clean and dry at all times.
- Table tops must be kept spotless, dirty cleaning cloths should never be used.
- Waste should be collected and placed in easily cleanable containers in a safe position.
- Cutlery should be carefully stored in racks or drawers with the handles facing in the same direction.
- Cups and containers used for serving or eating food should never be used to store or hold other substances, for example disinfectants and solvents.

TO DO

Draw up a rough sketch of your work area showing the location of fire exits, extinguishers, fire alarms and the assembly point. The next time there is a fire drill, time how long it takes you and your colleagues to reach the assembly point.